Emerging Economic Landscape of Saudi Arabia: Opportunities for India

Sameena Hameed

GULF STUDIES PROGRAMME
India Arab Cultural Centre
Jamia Millia Islamia

Emerging Economic Landscape of Saudi Arabia: Opportunities for India
Sameena Hameed

First Published 2015

ISBN 978-93-5002-389-1

Published by
AAKAR BOOKS
28 E Pocket IV, Mayur Vihar Phase I, Delhi 110 091
Phone: 011 2279 5505 Telefax: 011 2279 5641
aakarbooks@gmail.com; www.aakarbooks.com

In association with
India Arab Cultural Centre
Jamia Millia Islamia
New Delhi 110 025

Printed at
D.K. Fine Art Press, Delhi 110 052

Contents

Introduction

Saudi Arabia has been one of the fastest growing economies in the West Asia and North Africa (WANA) with average annual growth rate of 8.8 percent in the last decade.[1] Its economy still depends heavily on the oil sector. Oil revenue accounts for about 90.0 percent of total government revenues, oil exports account for about 88.0 percent of total export earnings, and the oil sector contributes about 35.0 percent to Gross Domestic Product (GDP).

The Kingdom of Saudi Arabia has the largest petroleum reserves in the world. It has an estimated proven oil reserve of about 264 billion barrels. Though, it has about eighty oil and gas fields, about 50 percent of its oil reserves are concentrated in eight oil fields.[2] It includes Ghawar, the world's largest oil field containing about 70 billion barrels of oil and Safaniya, the world's largest offshore oil field. Table 1 shows the production capacity of major oil fields in

1. Saad Alshahrani and Ali Alsadiq, 'Economic Growth and Government Spending in Saudi Arabia: An Empirical Investigation', *IMF Working Paper, WP/14/3* 2014, https://www.imf.org/external/pubs/ft/wp/2014/wp1403.pdf (accessed on 15 February 2015).
2. Michael O'Kane, *Doing Business in Saudi Arabia*, Tel Aviv, Al-Andalus Publishing, 2013, p. 5.

Saudi Arabia. The Kingdom produces variety of crude oils, heavy as well as extra light. About 65-70 percent of its total oil production capacity is of light gravity variety while the rest is either medium or heavy. It has substantial spare capacity of about 2.7 million barrels per day (mbpd) that can be brought online at short notice.[3]

Table 1: Major Oil Fields in Saudi Arabia

Major Oil Fields	*Location*	*Production/Capacity*
Ghawar	Onshore	5 mbpd of Arab Light crude
Safaniya	Offshore	1.5 mbpd of Arab Heavy crude
Khurais	Onshore	1.2 mbpd of Arab Light crude
Manifa	Offshore	0.9 mbpd of Arab Heavy crude oil after completion.
Shaybah	Onshore	0.75 mbpdof Arab Extra Light (after completion)
Qatif	Onshore	Capacity 500,000 bbl/d of Arab Light crude
Khursaniyah	Onshore	500,000 bbl/d Arab Light Crude
Zuluf	Offshore	450,000 bbl/d of Arab Medium crude
Abqaiq	Onshore	400,000 bbl/d Arab Extra Light crude

Source: Energy Information Administration (EIA).

The Saudi-Kuwait Neutral Zone (or the Divided Zone) contains an estimated 8 billion barrels of proven oil reserves that is shared equally between the two countries.[4] Crude oil production has been approximately 600,000 barrels per day

3. Ahmed Al-Darwish, Naif Alghaith and others, *Tackling Emerging Economic Challenges to Sustain Growth,* Washington DC, International Monetary Fund, 2015, p. 11.
4. Anthony H. Cordemen and Khalid R. Al Rodhan, *The Changing Dynamics of Energy in the Middle East*, Westport, USA, Greenwood Publishing Group, 2006, p. 19.

(bbl/d), although production declined slightly during the latter half of 2012. The three onshore fields (Wafra, Humma, and South Umm Gudair) had 2 billion barrels of proven reserves as estimated in 2012 and produce about 260,000 bbl/d of Arab Heavy oil. Bahrain and Saudi Arabia also share the 300,000 bbl/d production of the Abu Safah offshore field.

The oil fields in Saudi Arabia are mature and production from the major fields is declining. However, the estimates for rate of decline in oil production vary widely. Platts Oilgram in the year 2006 estimated that the decline rates for existing fields range from 6 to 8 percent annually, implying the requirement of about 700,000 bbl/d additional capacity each year to compensate for the natural decline. According to the Ministry of Petroleum and Mineral Resources the decline rates are closer to 2 to 3 percent per year. Saudi Aramco aims to conduct additional drilling at existing fields to help compensate for the natural decline from the mature fields, and the Kingdom is budgeting $20-$30 billion over the next 5 years to offset decline rates and maintain current capacity levels.

According to EIA estimates, Saudi Arabia is the fifth largest natural gas producer in the world after Russia, Iran, Qatar and the United States (US). Saudi Arabia (including the Neutral Zone it shares with Kuwait) is estimated to have proven natural gas reserves of 288 trillion cubic feet (tcf) at the end of 2012. Over the last decade, about 60 tcf of natural gas reserves were added in Saudi Arabia.[5] About 60 percent

5. *World Energy Resources 2013*, 23rd edition, London, World Energy Council Publication, 2013, http://www.worldenergy.org (accessed on 18 February 2015).

of gas reserves are composed of associated gas. About 33.3 percent of the gas reserves lies in the Ghawar oil field, while other significant gas reserves are in Safiniya and Zuluf oil fields.

There were plans to jointly develop with Kuwait, the offshore Dorra field (located in the Saudi-Kuwait Neutral Zone) but these have met with opposition because a small portion of that field is also claimed by Iran, which refers to it as the Arash field. Saudi Arabia reached an agreement with Kuwait in July 2000 to share Dorra output equally. According to Saudi Aramco, the field is estimated to contain non-associated natural gas reserves of between 35 and 60 tcf and the field is under seismic study. Recently, Kuwait and Saudi Arabia are locked in a fresh dispute and the work at the Dorra field has been halted due to differences between the two countries over the routing of the extracted gas. The production at offshore Khafji oilfield in the Neutral Zone was also halted due to emerging disagreement.[6]

6. Reem Shamseddine, 'Saudi Arabia, Kuwait Shared Zone Tensions underlie Oilfield Closure', *Reuters*, 21 October 2014, http://in.reuters.com/article/2014/10/21/saudi-kuwait-oil-disputes-idUSL6N0SF0BM20141021(accessed on 17 February 2015).

1

Oil and Gas Production and Processing Capacity

Saudi Arabia's oil and gas sector operations are dominated by the state-owned oil company, Saudi Aramco. Saudi Aramco is the world's largest oil company in terms of proven reserves and production of hydrocarbons. It operates the world's largest oil processing facility of more than 7 mbpd and crude stabilisation plant in the world at Abqaiq in eastern Saudi Arabia.[7] The plant processes the majority of Arab Extra Light and Arab Light crude oils, as well as Natural Gas Liquids (NGL). An extensive network of pipelines connects the plant to the ports of Ras al-Juaymah, RasTanura, and Yanbu (for NGL). Nearly two-third of Saudi crude is processed at Abqaiq before export or delivery to refineries.

According to the *Oil and Gas* Journal, Saudi Arabia has seven domestic refineries, with a combined crude throughput capacity of about 2.1 mbpd. It has approximately 2 mbpd of refining capacity overseas through joint and equity ventures in facilities in the US, China, South Korea, Japan and Philippines. In US, Saudi Aramco and Shell own

7. U. Aswathanarayana and Rao S. Divi, *Energy Portfolios*, Florida, CRC Press, 2009, p. 124.

three Motiva joint-venture refineries in Louisiana and Texas. The three facilities currently have a total capacity of about 740,000 bbl/d. Saudi Aramco owns 50 percent of Motiva through a subsidiary, Saudi Refining.[8]

8. *Shell Press Release*, 2008, http://wwwshell.com/content/dam/shell/static/usa/downloads/press/2008-news.pdf (accessed on 21 February 2015).

2

Saudi Arabia's Energy Trade

Saudi Arabia exported about 7.5 mbpd of crude oil in 2012. It earned about US$ 305,237,241,000 in the year 2012 (Annexure Table 1). It also exported petroleum products worth of $22,731,103,000 in the year 2012 and $8,155,722,000 worth of petroleum gases. East Asian countries received about 54 percent of Saudi Arabia's crude oil exports, as well as the majority of its refined petroleum products and NGL exports. Saudi Arabia exported an average of 1.4 mbpd of total petroleum liquids to the United States in the year 2012, accounting for 16 percent of total US crude oil imports. Saudi Arabia ranked second after Canada as a petroleum exporter to the US. The major Saudi consumers and their respective shares in the total oil exports in the year 2013 were Japan (15.7 percent), China (13.9 percent), South Korea (11.6 percent), and India (10.6 percent) (Annexure Table 4).

The rising domestic energy consumption in the country has also led to increasing imports (Annexure Table 2). In the year 2010, it imported $152,598,000 worth of petroleum products, which increased to $1,835,598,000 in the year 2013. It also imports residual petroleum products like petroleum jelly, bituminous, petroleum coke along with coal. The relative shares of the countries supplying energy products to Saudi Arabia are India (63.1 percent), Italy (10.1 percent),

Oman (5 percent), and Singapore (3.6 percent) (Annexure Table 3).

3

Investment in Energy Sector

Saudi Arabia has an investment plan of about US$ 125 billion for its upstream and downstream oil projects over the next five years. Saudi Aramco has already embarked on capital spending program of more than $100bn, which is the largest in its history. Saudi Arabia invested about $17bn for developing the Manifa offshore oil field to raise output of heavy crude, which is thicker and more difficult to refine. The company is planning three refineries to process the blend, which is generally priced lower in international markets compared to lighter crudes. Saudi Aramco has also awarded Saipem an Engineering Procurement and Construction (EPC) contract to expand the onshore production centres at the Khurais, Mazajili and Abu Jifan oil fields. The construction of new facilities will enable additional 300,000 bbl/d to be produced from the Khurais field, while the installation of new satellite facilities will restore production of 200,000 bbl/d from the Abu Jifan and Mazalij fields.

Saudi Aramco has an investment plan of about $90 bn to expand its refining and petrochemical capacity to emerge as the largest producer and exporter of petrochemicals within the next decade. It is integrating its refinery projects with large petrochemicals complexes, often described as petrochemical cities. Saudi Aramco Total Refining and Petrochemical Company (SATORP) in Jubail is a 400,000 bbl/d joint venture with France's Total. It will be an export refinery, processing mainly Arab Heavy crude, and producing diesel and jet fuel. Yanbu Aramco Sinopec Refining Company (YASREF) Limited, a joint venture with Chinese Petrochemical Corporation (Sinopec) is designed to process about 400,000 bbl/d of Arab Heavy crude oil from the planned Manifa oil development. Jazan refinery project with an estimated capacity of about 400,000 bbl/d is being developed in Southwest Saudi Arabia to process majority of country's crude oil grades by late 2016. Saudi Arabia has also initiated a number of clean fuel projects to provide more ultra-low sulphur diesel.

Saudi Arabia is investing to develop its natural gas deposits to run power plants, refining and petrochemical plants. The Kingdom used 8.1 billion cubic feet per day (bcf/d) of gas. To meet growing domestic demand for additional production, the Petroleum Ministry and Saudi Aramco announced a $9-billion strategy to add 50 tcf of non-associated gas reserves by 2016 through new discoveries and another 50 tcf of associated gas reserves. The high sulphur content of these gases, as well as the offshore location significantly increase the cost of their development.

The Saudi domestic natural gas market, traditionally the sole domain of Saudi Aramco, is slowly being opened to private investment both in exploration and distribution. The foreign consortium exploring onshore gas and condensate (NGLs) in the Rub al-Khali (Empty Quarters), was heralded as the first foreign investment in Saudi Arabia's upstream energy sector. Royal Dutch/Shell, France's Total, Russia's Lukoil and China's Sinopec were awarded stakes in the gas projects in the Empty Quarters. But soon they left the project. The officials were of the view that it was not economically feasible due to high content of hydrogen sulphide in the sour gas located in the area. Besides, the known gas resources in the Rub al-Khali desert cannot be developed until the government raises the domestic gas price.

Aramco is also looking for gas deposits in the Red Sea. New gas field was discovered by Saudi Aramco in the Red Sea, 26 km North West of the port of Daba. Gas flowed at the rate of 10 million cubic feet a day (mcf/d) at a test well at the depth of 17,700 feet.[9] Aramco is also focusing on unconventional resources. Saudi oil minister Ali Al-Naimi had estimated that the country has unconventional gas reserves at over 600 tcf, more than double the proven conventional reserves of 288 tcf.

Saudi deserts may hold about 645 tcf of technically recoverable shale gas, which is the fifth largest deposits in the world after China, US, Argentina and Mexico, according to estimates by Baker Hughes Inc.[10]

Natural gas and NGLs processing capacity is being expanded from 9.3 bcf/d to 12.5 bcf/d at Khursaniyah, Hawiyah, Ju'aymah, Yanbu, and Khurais. Saudi Arabia is also building a 2.5 bcf/d Wasit gas plant, which will be one of the largest gas plants in the Kingdom. This plant will receive gas from the Arabiyah and Hasbah fields.

Saudi Aramco has awarded contract to Chinese firm

---

9. 'Saudi Arabia Finds New Gas Fields in Red Sea', *Reuters*, 9 October 2012, http://www.reuters.com/article/2012/10/09/saudi-gas-discovery-idUSL6E8L9O3020121009 (accessed on 25 February 2015).
10. Syed R. Husain, 'KSA Shifting to Unconventional Gas Resources', *Saudi Gazette*, 3 August 2014, http://www.saudi gazette.com.sa/ accessed on 2 March 2015.

Shandong Electric Power Construction Corporation (SEPCO) to design and build a Master Gas System Booster Gas Compression station. The first two phases involve the installation of pipe branching off and along the East-West pipeline, construction of three compression station facilities and residential facilities along with an integrated waste-heat recovery system for power generation. MGS was built in the mid-1970s to gather and process associated gas from oil wells for domestic industries. The project will facilitate delivery of gas to the western region, including the King Abdullah Economic City, Petro Rabigh and an independent power plant with an estimated 9.6 bcf/d of gas and will further increase to 12.5 bcf/d by 2018 under a second phase. Saudi Aramco has also awarded a front-end engineering design (FEED) and project management services contract for its Fadhili gas plant project to Foster Wheeler. Fadhili gas plant in the eastern province is estimated to have total processing capacity of 1.5 billion standard cubic feet per day of non-associated gas.

Saudi Arabia faces imminent challenge in generating fuel resources to meet its power demands. Power capacity in the country was about 49,138 mega watt (mw) by the end of 2010, growing at a 10 year compound annual growth rate (cagr) of 6.7 percent.[11] The total consumption and peak load demand grew at 10 year (cagr) of 6.4 per cent and 7.7 per cent, respectively, amounting to 212,263 gw and 45,661 mw.[12]

Saudi Arabia needs to expand its power capacity and networks to support its ambitious industrialisation plan, as

11. 'GCC Energy Sector – Quarterly Review 2011', *Ventures Middle East*, 2011, http://www.pipelineme.com/media/797133/gcc-energy-december-2011.pdf (accessed on 3 December 2014).
12. 'Greater Power Generation Key to Sustain Kingdom's Growth', *Arab News*, 15 December 2011, http//www.arabnews.com (accessed on 15 March 2015).

well as cater to the demand of its growing population. However, the critical challenge in the execution of the commissioned projects lies in the artificially low tariffs in a highly regulated sector, which not only impedes profit margins but also leads to inefficient use of electricity. The Electricity and Water Ministry had revised the tariffs in July 2010. The industrial and governmental consumer groups were subjected to higher rates, therefore cross subsidising residential users, who account for the largest share of demand. Another challenge is the large amount of funding required for Saudi Electricity Company (SEC) projects and Independent Power producers (IPPs). The total expenditure for upgrading the transmission network is estimated at SR 12.95bn annually over the next five years. SEC is estimated to spend SR 7bn annually over the same period for expanding, maintaining and improving its distribution network.

The power sector consumes huge amount of petroleum. The rising petroleum consumption is a major challenge, as the government aims to reserve crude oil for export. Substantial investment in solar would save the country's oil for export. The government is targeting 41 gwh of solar capacity within two decades, which is estimated to generate a surplus of about 523,000 bbl/d for export.[13] The Kingdom is also tapping into other alternative sources of energy, such as nuclear and wind power.

---

13. Wael Mahdi, 'Mecca Seeks to Lead Saudi Arabia's Solar Energy', *Bloomberg News*, 23 September 2012, http://www.bloomberg.com/news/2012-09-23/mecca-seeks-to-lead-saudi-arabia-s-solar-energy-expansion.html (accessed on 21 February 2015).

King Abdullah City for Atomic and Renewable Energy (KA CARE), the apex organisation for promoting alternative energy has set ambitious target of sourcing 20 percent (equivalent to 18,000 megawatts) of its electricity demand to be met from renewable energy sources by 2030. Saudi Arabia is already experimenting with solar power to desalinate water. KA CARE has installed nationwide stations to measure the ability to produce electricity from the sun, wind, geothermal and waste sources. It has also launched a Renewable Energy Atlas for Saudi Arabia. KA CARE also plans to build the country's first fleet of 16 nuclear reactors by 2030. In February 2011, the country agreed with France to cooperate in the development of nuclear energy in addition to utilising geothermal, wind and solar power.

The Kingdom plans to seek investment of about $109 billion to create a solar industry.[14] It has allocated US$3 billion to produce solar energy panels in Jubail and Yanbu plants. KACARE is commissioned by the SEC to construct solar power plants. The stations to be built in the Qaisomah, Rafha, Wadi Al Dawaser, Mahd Al Dahab and Sharourah regions are scheduled to complete by the end of 2015. It is estimated that the five plants will add between 700 mw and 1000 mw to the grid.[15] It is still to be known whether the projects would be operated directly by state agencies or in partnership with private firms.

---

14. 'Saudi Arabia Explores Potential $109 bn Solar Industry', *Al-Arabiya News*, 3 July 2013, http//www.english.alarabia.net (accessed on 24 April 2015).
15. 'Saudi Arabia Powering Up', *Oxford Business Group*,18 November 2014, http://www.oxfordbusinessgroup.com/news/saudi-arabia-powering (accessed on 16 April 2015).

A Riyadh-based company ACWA Power International has robust plans to push solar power throughout Saudi Arabia and has international renewable energy acquisitions to further its expertise in the industry. It has invested in power plants in Jordan, Oman, Turkey, Morocco and some African and southeast Asian countries to further their skills and is planning to add solar assets, both at home and abroad to triple production capacity to 38,000 mw by 2017. ACWA Power is seeking to arrange finance for $15 billion worth of projects, nearly half of which are in renewable energy.[16] It is also expected to win the contract for building a 100 mw power plant in Mecca. ACWA Power's success demonstrates enormous renewable energy capabilities emerging in the WANA region in solar and wind power projects.

Since the year 2009, the King Abdul Aziz City for Science and Technology (KACST) has been working in collaboration with IBM on advanced photovoltaic (pv). The research has led to the development of solar power desalination plants and two pilot operations at Al-Khafji and Rabigh. There are already some small-scale solar power stations operating as a result of initiatives taken in developing the renewable energy program in early 2013. Saudi Arabia has at present 3 mw of solar capacity, which ranks it below Algeria, Egypt, Morocco, Tunisia, and the UAE but the status is set to change in the coming decades. Although, Saudi Arabia has the financial capacity to undertake, the renewable energy projects yet reliance on foreign experts is detrimental to its

16. 'Saudi Arabia's ACWA Power Shifts toward Renewable Energy', *Emirates GBC News Letter*, vol. IV, no. 11, 2014, http://emiratesgbc.org/newsletter/volume-iv-issue-11/ (accessed on 17 January 2015).

long-term success. The Kingdom is completely dependent on foreign consultants, scientists and experts especially in their nuclear program.

At present, Saudi Arabia does not have an extensive solar energy service segment as most of the material and technology are being imported. It provides lucrative opportunities for private investors to enter the industry, by forming partnerships with established international renewable energy service providers. SunEdison, a US firm was reported to be in talks over the establishment of a $6.4bn integrated PV manufacturing complex to cater to the domestic market as well as the regional market in the WANA region.[17]

The daily electricity demand of remote posts, highway family rests, remotely located mosques, small-sized villages and border areas are usually met through expensive and unreliable diesel generators that are transported at regular intervals to these areas. A minimum of $1 billion is spent every month on diesel imports to the Kingdom.[18] An off-grid solution is much more economical than delivering electricity to a small area by conventional means. Saudi Arabia is looking to offset diesel consumption with off-grid solar photovoltaic applications and hybrid solutions. It offers significant opportunities for local developers and suppliers to power remote residential and industrial areas through

---

17. 'Saudi Arabia Powering Up', *Oxford Business Group*,18 November 2014.
18. Vahid Fotuhi, 'Concern over Saudi Arabia's Summer Diesel Consumption Surge', *The National Business*, 5 July 2013, http://www.thenational.ae/business/industry-insights/energy/concern-over-saudi-arabias-summer-diesel-consumption-surge (accessed on 11 February 2015).

hybrid designs, including solar-powered desalination and cooling.

Saudi Aramco and SEC are aiming to replace about 300 mw of diesel generation in off-grid locations with solar PVs. A 500-kilowatt solar power plant, first remotely installed and grid-connected in the Kingdom is constructed on Saudi Arabia's Farasan Island near Jeddah.[19] The plant is estimated to substitute 28,000 barrels of diesel in its life span. The Nofa Equestrian Resort located 85 km west of Riyadh has functional 1 mw concentrator photovoltaic (CPV) plant based on the hybrid concept, which is offsetting the 14 mw diesel generator that the resort is using. Companies like FAS Energy are preparing to supply the local market with hybrid solutions. In January 2013, Chinese firm ReneSola was awarded its first contract in the Gulf region to supply 15 kilowatts of solar modules for use in an off-grid power plant.[20] The project was given by Taibah University in Medina.

Flexible power generation, power networks, demand side management and energy storage are some of the challenges encountered in the development of solar energy. Saudi Arabia is now in a position to offer one of the lowest cost of energy (LCOE), with solar power price fallen more than four times than in 2009. Solar power costs have declined

---

19. A.H. Almasoud and Hatim M. Gandayh, 'Future of Solar Energy in Saudi Arabia', *Journal of King Saud University*, 2014, http://dx.doi.org/10.1016/j.jksues.2014.03.007 (accessed 27 March 2015).
20. Nilima Chouhury, 'ReneSola Enters Saudi Market with 15KW Contract', 14 January 2014, http://wwwtech.org/news/order_focus_renesola_enters_saudi_market_with_15kw_contract (accessed 18 February 2015).

due to lower module prices, lower system costs and increased competition at the development and EPC level. The financing costs have also come down as investors have become acquainted with the low-risk profile of solar assets. The Saudi competency for reaching a record solar LCOE was also demonstrated in the 100 mw PV Independent Power Project tender issued by Dubai's state utility Dubai Electricity and Water Authority (DEWA). ACWA Power bid an unprecedented low of 5.98 US$ cents/kwh.[21] As an additional achievement, ACWA Power not only provided the lowest bid, but also provided alternative bids to immediately build 1,000 mw at a tariff of 5.4 cents/kwh for the 1,000 mw variant. The extremely low winning bid established world record for the lowest cost of solar electricity at a time when the recent, when the recent records in India and Brazil have been set around the 8–9 cents/kwh mark. The low tariff bid in a fully commercial, unsubsidised setting, dispels the prevailing misconceptions in the region about the allegedly high cost of PV and should provide a boost to other governmental procurement programs in Saudi Arabia.

21. 'Dubai Doubles Capacity of Mega Solar Park', *Gulf News*, 15 January 2015, http://gulfnews.com/news/gulf/uae/environment/dubai-doubles-capacity-of-mega-solar-park-1.1441860 (accessed 12 December 2014).

4

Non-Energy Sector: Trade and Investment

The private sector has now a larger role in the Saudi economy accounting for 48 percent of the GDP. The Kingdom is trying to diversify the economy and is focusing on power generation, telecommunications, natural gas exploration, and petrochemical sectors. It is investing billions of dollars to build four new 'economic cities' or smart cities as a part of economic diversification. The smart cities are aimed to create a knowledge economy that will provide the Kingdom's younger population with the skills required for professional and senior-level jobs. Saudi Arabia General Investment Authority (SAGIA) expects the economic cities to contribute US $150 billion to GDP and create more than 1 million jobs by 2020.

Saudi Arabia acceded to the World Trade Organisation (WTO) in 2005 to attract foreign investment. The government envisages the economic cities in different regions of the country as foreign investment enclaves and plans to spend $373 billion between 2010 and 2014 on social development and infrastructure projects. The economic cities are:

1. King Abdullah Economic City in Rabigh focusing on port and logistics, light industry and services;
2. Prince Abdulaziz bin Musaid Economic City in Hael

emerging as a new hub for logistics in the region being located at the crossroads of trade and transportation routes for West Asia. It focuses on logistics, agribusiness, minerals and construction material;

3. Knowledge Economic City in Madinah focusing on knowledge based industries with an Islamic focus and services;
4. Jazan Economic City focusing on energy and labor intensive industries.

The Jubail industrial city on the Arabian Gulf has dozens of factories and industrial facilities including a desalination plant, a seaport, a vocational training institute and a college. The Yanbu industrial city on the Red Sea has a modern port, refineries, a petrochemical complex and many manufacturing and support enterprises. The Saudi Arabian Basic Industries Corporation (SABIC) was set up in 1976 to create non-oil industrial facilities that use as feedstock natural gas and NGLs manufactured by the oil industry.

Saudi Arabia has made significant progress in liberalising investment and business regulations for foreign firms. National treatment of foreign investment has been established. Hundred percent foreign investments are allowed except for a negative list and the sectors having caps. The negative list has been subsequently reduced. Foreign Investment Act 2000 in Saudi Arabia guarantees the repatriation of profit and capital and streamlines the investment process through a one-stop investment agency. Gas extraction and mining were opened to foreign investment in 2003. Oil exploration, drilling and extraction remain off limits. The tax rate on foreign companies has been more than halved from 45 percent to 20 percent. Saudi Arabia is also considering plan to set up free trade zone. The

World Bank Ease of Doing Business 2014 report ranks Saudi Arabia as the 44th most attractive business destination in the world.

Saudi Arabia aims to boost petrochemical exports to act as engine of growth and employment. Like other Gulf Cooperation Council (GCC) countries, it faces natural gas shortages as new power plants compete for gas supplies. Besides, naptha based petrochemical plants have larger and more complex product options like aromatic based chemicals and derivatives while ethane based plants can generally produce olefins. Hence, there is a perceptible shift towards heavier feed stock and integration of petroleum refineries and petrochemical plants like Petro Rabigh's integrated refinery. It also aims to move up the petrochemical value chain. Saudi Arabia in the industrial cities of Yanbu and Jubail look forward for value added specialty and performance chemicals and further down to the product chains, plastics and energy intensive industries such as minerals and metals. Their consumer product cluster industries initiative offer business opportunities for investors in consumer goods, automotives, construction materials, packaging and metals processing.

Saudi Arabia has already developed some export potential in many product categories. Annexure Table 5 shows the value and percentage share of Saudi exports. It exported $11,339,317,000 worth of plastics in the year 2010, which increased to $17,029,840,000 in 2013. It exported about $7,440,552,000 of organic chemicals in 2010, which increased to $13,210,626,000 in the year 2013. Electronic, electrical equipments exports were about $1,058,756,000 in 2010 and it increased to $1,560,284,000 in 2013. Saudi Arabia is rich in all grades of potash. But its fertilizer exports have not significantly increased. SABIC has to face tough competition to enter the Asian markets mainly due to strong presence of SINOPEC, Reliance and Industries Qatar in these areas. The ranking of importing countries for Saudi Arabia is given in Annexure Table 6.

Saudi Arabia, due to its massive diversification programme is a large importer of engineering, automotive, electrical and electronic goods (Annexure Table 7). It imported nearly $26 bn of machinery items, $17 bn of electronic, electrical equipments and $19 bn worth of metallic products in the year 2013. The shares of machinery items, vehicles and electrical and electronic equipments in the total imports were 15.9 percent, 14.3 percent and 10.8 percent respectively. (Annexure Table 7). The ranking of exporting countries to Saudi Arabia is given in Annexure Table 8.

Food and agriculture sectors are among the fastest growing sectors in Saudi Arabia, which have witnessed rapid expansion, research and development. The sectors have better immunity against economic cycles in term of volumetric growth because of strong spending habits of nationals. There are about ten parent foreign companies in these sectors and Switzerland is the leading foreign investor.

Saudi Arabia will be experiencing a sharp increase in health care needs due to growing and ageing population and a rise in chronic non-communicable lifestyle diseases. The country currently imports about 95 percent of its pharmaceutical requirements mostly from the US and Europe. The government is trying to boost domestic drug manufacturing by entering into joint ventures and licensing deals with multinational pharmaceutical companies. It allows 100 percent foreign investment in the sector. Pharmaceuticals multinational firms do not have manufacturing facilities in smaller GCC countries and operate through representative offices in Saudi Arabia or the UAE. Since Saudi Arabia became trade-related aspects of Intellectual Property Rights (TRIPS) compliant in 2009, and already has a drug manufacturing and certification base, investors are trying to spread operations from there. There are five parent foreign companies investing in health and other services in the Kingdom.[22]

Saudi Arabia awarded its largest construction contract by value of about $42 bn in 2013, compared to $17 bn in 2012. It has also prioritised providing affordable housing under its Five Year Development Plan for 2010-2014. During the plan, it aims to build at least 1 million affordable housing units across the Kingdom and allocate a budget of about US$ 82 billion to fund housing projects across the country. Recent measures to boost real estate investment include the creation of a new Ministry of Housing, the passing of the mortgage law in July 2012 and increase housing finance for Saudi citizens in conformity with Shariah laws and covering issues such as registration of mortgages, financial leasing and enforcement and real estate funding. Major Saudi cities are forecast to have strong demand for both residential and commercial real estate as local banks are now licensed to increase property lending.

---

22. International Trade Centre Database, http://www.intracen.org (accessed on 11 April 2015).

5

Sustainable Development in Saudi Arabia

Saudi Arabia is projecting itself as 'the hub of sustainable energy'. The buildings are amongst the highest consumer of energy. The Saudi Centre for Energy Efficiency (SCEE) estimated that buildings consume about 80 percent of total electricity produced in the country, about 50 percent of which is used for air conditioning. Figure 1 shows the energy usage in Saudi Arabia. In contrast in the US; Heat, Ventilation and Air Conditioning Systems (HVAC) use 31.4 percent of total energy consumption.

Saudi Green Building Council (SGBC) since its establishment in the year 2010 has been promoting and facilitating the construction of green buildings in the Kingdom for sustainable use of energy and water resources. It increases public awareness, provides training and education, facilitates the construction industry to comply to the green building requirements. It encourages building material manufacturers and suppliers to produce and supply environmentally responsible products, promote green labelling, adapt, develop and operate local green building rating system that meet the local environmental requirements.

Figure 1: Energy Usage in Saudi Arabia

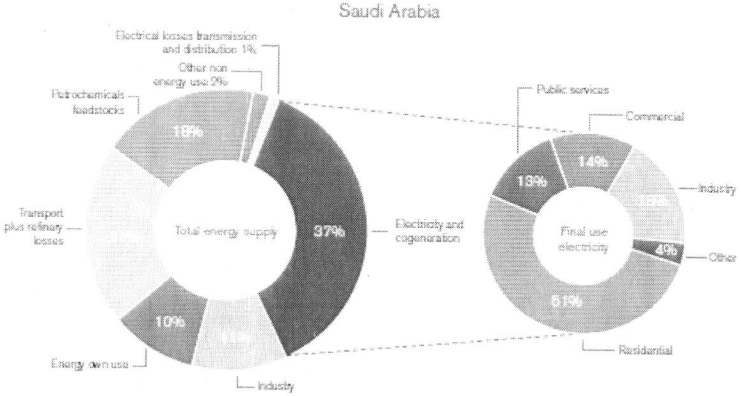

Source: Glada Lahn and Others, 'Saving Oil and Gas in the Gulf', *A Chatham House Report*, August 2013.

There are few stellar examples of green building architectures in Saudi Arabia. King Abdullah University for Science and Technology (KAUST) campus was awarded Saudi Arabia's first-ever Leadership in Energy and Environmental Design (LEED) Platinum rating in 2010. The roof of the building is capable of carrying 12,000 square meters of solar thermal and solar PV arrays capable of producing 3,300 megawatt hours of clean energy every year catering to 7.8 percent of the energy requirements on-site.[23]

The campus used recycled content in most of its construction material and diverted more than 75 percent of its construction waste from landfills. The buildings have thermal massing systems, sunlight-reflecting material, water-conserving fixtures, renewable energy generation and solar chimneys that produce cool breeze for the building air conditioning.

23. KAUST, http://www.kaust.edu.sa/green-campus-sustainable-development.html (accessed on 28 May 2015).

The building development project at Al Khobar will be another prominent LEED certified building. The building generates its own power by using solar cells that are laminated within the glass of the curtain wall. Passive heating and cooling systems will be operational through the use of double glazed multi-ventilation windows and cavity walls. Waste water recycle systems, green roofs, living walls, use of recycled material and provisions for passive storage of heating and heat recovery are other sustainable features.

The King Abdullah International Gardens (KAIG) in Riyadh, which will house the world's largest indoor garden won the 2010 coveted Cityscape Award for Real Estate in the Middle East and North Africa in the 'Best Sustainable Development' category. Among others are the residential community for the King Abdullah Petroleum Studies and Research Centre (KAPSARC) with more than eighty two LEED Gold certified villas, which is the first and largest project to achieve LEED for home certification outside North America.[24] The King Abdullah Financial District Conference Centre used about 50 percent of the recycled building material, besides having other sustainable features.[25]

The construction industry has recently started improving with many new sustainable projects in the design and construction phase. However, the market for green buildings is still nascent and lacks the proper infrastructure and incentives to enforce such schemes. There is lack of interest by the client due to the higher costs of environment-friendly

24. HOK, http://www.hok.com/about/news/2012/10/31/kapsarc-reaches-leed-for-homes-milestone/ (accessed on 11 April 2015).
25. *The Report: Saudi Arabia 2013*, London, Oxford Business Group, 2013, p. 297.

products. Unless the government develops and strictly enforces green regulations, such as Abu Dhabi's Estidama Pearl Rating Systems, rather than voluntary ratings (LEED), it will be very difficult for Saudi Arabia to lay out strong incentives and foundations that ensure greener and energy efficient building constructions and operations. The scarcity of Saudi engineers specialised in green building has crippled the sector's growth. There are only about 150 Saudi engineers specialised in green building construction.[26]

The Council of Saudi Chambers and the SGBC have agreed to launch an eco-friendly joint venture following King Abdullah's directives in promoting the green sector in the Kingdom. The first Saudi Green Building Forum for green buildings was held in 2010. It led to achieving approximately 60 percent of the plans and recommendations suggested by the forum, including registering 160 projects in Riyadh, Makkah, Madinah and the Eastern Province. A green building division for Saudi engineers, which included 700 specialists was formed.

Since 2010, Saudi building code mandates thermal insulation against heat for all new buildings, which has proved to reduce energy demand for villas by 30 to 40 percent. However, due to lack of monitoring, new buildings continue to be constructed without stipulated insulation. Collaboration between ministries, municipal governments and electricity authorities strengthens the potential for enforcement of building regulations. All the proposed buildings in Riyadh must be checked from the planning to the end of construction to verify installation of the correct

---

26. 'Green Building Technology in Spotlight', *Arab News*, 7 September 2013, http:/ / www.arabnews.com (accessed on 13 January 2014).

thermal insulation before the building can be connected to the grid electricity supply.

In early March 2014, the Presidency of Meteorology and Environment (PME) announced a decree giving all companies five years to meet new air, water and noise pollution standards.[27] Companies refusing to comply with the new standards within five years will see their projects shut down or suspended for three months. The decree shows a formal commitment to the Saudi Green Building Forum's initiatives.

27. D.C. McCullough, 'Saudi Arabia's Green Decree Brings Hopes of Sustainability', *The Guardian*, 12 May 2014, http://www.the.guardian.com (accessed on 13 March 2015).

6

Saudi Arabia in Regional Economic Setting

Saudi Arabia is the largest economy of the GCC economic bloc. It contributes about 49 percent of the total GDP of the economic bloc and 67 percent of the total population. It is gradually integrating into the regional market through trade and investment. It has set up nearly 83 parent companies in the developing countries and many countries in the WANA region are the leading host for Saudi investment (Annexure Table 17). SABIC, Saudi Cables Company, Ara Group International Holding Ltd are some of the leading investors in the region. SABIC is owned 70 percent by the Saudi government and 30 percent by shareholders from the six GCC countries. Saudi Arabia has invested in wholesale and retail trade, business activities, chemicals, transport, storage and communications, electrical and electronic equipments, finance, construction and metal and metal products.

Massive construction projects estimated to be about $1trillion in active phase and large industrial projects have led to huge demand for metallic products especially steel and aluminium in the GCC region. The region currently consumes up to 400,000 tonnes of aluminium annually. Saudi Arabia is the only country in the region which is in a position to substantially increase production to meet the strong regional demand for metallic products.

Annexure Table 9 shows Saudi Arabia's exports to the West Asia and Table 10 shows the ranking of West Asian countries importing from Saudi Arabia. Plastic products, electronic and electrical equipments, metallic products are some of the prominent exports to the region. The exports to the region were $19,504,601,000 in the year 2013 (Annexure Table 9). Jordan, Egypt, Oman, Turkey and Qatar are among the leading importers in the region (Annexure Table 10). Table 9 also shows the imports of West Asia from the world signifying its growing market potential. Annexure Table 11 shows the products imported by Saudi Arabia from the region. Metals and metallic products are the leading imports from the region. Turkey, Oman, Egypt, Qatar and Jordan are the leading suppliers of Saudi imports from the region (Annexure Table 12).

Regional energy cooperation is also emerging. Saudi Arabia and the UAE have agreed to cooperate to develop renewable energy and clean technology in the region. Masdar in Abu Dhabi and the KA CARE signed an agreement to jointly invest in clean energy projects besides collaborating on research and development of advanced clean energy technologies including solar, wind and water. Cross-regional electricity trade can be one of the most effective ways to make renewable energy investments more profitable and attractive to a growing number of investors in the West Asian region. The Gulf Cooperation Council Interconnection Authority (GCCIA) has constructed and commissioned a 400kv interconnection grid between Kuwait, Saudi Arabia, Bahrain, Qatar and UAE that includes 900 km of overhead lines, seven 400kv substations, a 1800mw three-pole back-to-back HVDC converter station and a submarine cable to Bahrain.[28]

28. Tawfiq M. Aljohani, and Abdullah M. Alzahrani, 'The Operations of the GCCIA HVDC Project and Its Potential Impact on Electric Power Systems of the Region', *International Journal of Electronics and Electrical Engineering*, vol. 2, no. 3, September 2014, p. 207.

7

India-Saudi Economic Relations

India's merchandise import from Saudi Arabia was about $28,423,659,000 in the year 2011 and it increased to $36,596,585,000 in 2013 (Annexure Table 13). The petroleum imports constituted about 90 percent of India's total imports from Saudi Arabia. Other categories of imports, which registered a substantial increase are plastics and articles thereof, pearls, precious stones and fertilizers.

Annexure Table 14 shows the composition of Saudi imports from India. The main imports are cereals, electrical, electronic equipment, and machineries and their relative shares in total imports were 18 percent, 10.5 percent and 9.2 percent respectively in the year 2013. Annexure Table 14 also shows that there has been a substantial increase in some categories of imports viz, vehicles other than railway, tramway, mineral fuels and their relative shares in the total imports from India have also increased. However, pharmaceuticals figures in top ten Saudi imports and top ten India's exports but does not figure in top ten items of India's exports to Saudi Arabia.

Annexure Table 8 shows that India ranked fourth leading exporter to Saudi Arabia in the year 2010 with the share of about 4.8 percent in latter's total merchandise imports. It again ranked fourth in the year 2013 but its share increased to 8.6 percent. Table 14 shows that Saudi Arabia's merchandise imports from India were about $4,231,442,000 in the year 2011, which increased to $5,771,803,000 in 2013. India ranked as fifth largest importing market after China, US, Japan, Korea in the year 2010 and 2013 (Annexure Table 6). However its relative share increased from 8.5 percent in 2010 to 10.2 percent in 2013.

India imports crude oil, petroleum gases and petroleum products from Saudi Arabia (Annexure Table 15). Crude oil imports were $23,513,374,000 in the year 2011, which increased to $31,202,907,000 in 2013. The Indian exports of energy products to Saudi Arabia have increased from $1,239,673,000 in the year 2011 to $6,877,519,000 in 2013. The product wise details of India's energy exports to Saudi Arabia are given in Annexure Table 16.

Indian investment in Saudi Arabia has crossed $1.6 billion, SAGIA is reported to have issued about 426 licences to the Indian companies for joint ventures or hundred percent Indian owned companies in various projects in industries, in services and in agriculture in Saudi Arabia. In addition, several Indian companies are working in Saudi Arabia in the areas of construction, IT, software development, designing, consultancy, financial services etc. According to Department of Industrial Policy and Promotion, Saudi Arabia has invested in India about US $ 47 million between April 2000 to October 2014 in Saudi-Indian joint ventures in diverse fields such as paper manufacture, chemicals, granite processing, industrial products and machinery, metallurgical industries, stationery, granite slabs, asbestos, cement and computer software specially for health and financial sectors. Indian IT companies are already involved with a growing number of

Saudi companies that have outsourced their IT requirements. The Indian firms have supplied high quality products and skills at a fraction of the international cost. Saudi investment in India is much below potential. It has set up in Bengaluru a technical centre with an investment of about $150 million.[29]

Saudi Aramco has awarded Larsen and Tubro a contract to build facilities, including a gas processing plant for its Midyan gas field.[30] The project will include building two pipelines of 98 km length to deliver gas and hydrocarbon liquids to a power plant near the western city of Al-Helal enabling efficient generation of power and save burning of diesel. Essar Projects has also won a $54 million maiden contract from Saudi Aramco to upgrade crude stabilisation unit at Abqaiq plant in Shaybah, one of the largest oilfields in the world. The company is already executing five other projects in the region in the hydrocarbon sector.

India is the fourth largest energy consumer in the world. Its per capita energy consumption is one third the global average. As the second fastest growing economy, its energy consumption is poised to increase exponentially. India's energy future is that of heavy import dependence. The energy demand has been growing at 6-7 percent. In December 2008, Government of India approved an Integrated Energy Policy (IEP) for the country projecting 100 percent electrification of all households and cooking fuel requirement of LPG for 1.5 billion persons at around 55

29. 'India-Saudi Arabia Economic and Commercial Brief', *Indian Embassy*, 15 January 2015, http://www.indianembassy.org (accessed on 19 March 2015).
30. Reem Shamseddine, 'Aramco Awards Midyan Gas Project to L&T', *Reuters*, 21 May 2012, http://www.reuters.com (accessed on 14 May 2015).

million tonnes of oil equivalent by 2020. The IEP estimated that the India's primary energy supply will need to increase by 4 to 5 times and its electricity generation capacity by 6 to 7 times of its 2003-04 levels to deliver a sustained growth rate of 9 percent through 2031-32. It implies an annual growth rate of 5.8 percent of primary energy supply. Oil and gas accounts for nearly 45 percent of India's total energy consumption. The petroleum and natural gas reserves in India at the current reserve to production ratio would last about 21 years and 29 years respectively. India imports 80 percent of its oil needs and most of oil imports comes from geopolitically unstable regions of the world. The demand for oil is projected to reach 370 million tonnes by the year 2025. India should produce at least 110 million tonnes per year. To maintain this level, there is a need to add 60 million tonnes of oil every year to the existing production level. The demand for natural gas is estimated to be 220 million cubic metres (mcm) per day, compared to supply (including LNG) of around 142 mcm per day. The demand, according to the Ministry of Petroleum and Natural Gas is expected reach 280 mcm per day by 2016, against the forecast domestic supply of 190 mcm per day.

Saudi Arabia is the largest exporter of oil to India. Nevertheless, the trends of domestic energy consumption in Saudi Arabia and the challenges facing its energy sector open vital avenues of energy cooperation between the two nations. Saudi economy is often adversely affected by oil price fluctuations in the international market. With the decline of oil demand in the Western markets, Saudi Arabia is locking Asian markets by long term trade contracts and investment in their refineries. Therefore, there is a need for a revitalisation of Strategic Energy Partnership that was signed between King Abdullah and Indian Prime Minister Manmohan Singh in the year 2006.

India's total per annum refining capacity is expected to grow from 2.9 mbpd to 4.6 mbpd in few years. Indian refineries can refine heavy crude oil to produce light products with sulphur as low as 10 parts per million (ppm). Only Japan, Taiwan and South Korea have been able to refine petroleum products with zero sulphur content. Indian refineries have made large investments in technologies to make cleaner fuels and are expected to gain greater global market share and good refinery margins.[31] Indian oil companies like Oil India Corporation Limited (OIC) holds patents for cost effective non-conventional desulphurisation process. Indian petroleum products have been exported to America and European countries. Therefore, Indo-Saudi joint ventures in oil refineries is a mutual win win situation and would be able to meet international quality standards with freight advantage for exports to developed countries in comparison to refineries in Japan and Korea. The synergetic benefit of this cooperation has a positive spill over effect in the petrochemical sector, which will be increasingly integrated with the refining sector and therefore will be affected by oil price cycles.

India's competence in building and managing integrated petroleum refinery and petrochemical plants as well competence in whole range of chemicals creates business opportunities and capacity building in value added specialty and performance chemicals. India's chemical industry is the

31. 'Refining Margins under Pressure to 2015', *Hydrocarbon processing.com*, http://www.hydrocarbonprocessing.com/Article/2837639/Refining-margins-under-pressure-to-2015.html (accessed on 15 April 2014).

twelfth largest in the world and third largest in Asia in terms of volume and is valued at US$35 billion. A significant share of the industry is of high value chemicals. Specialty chemicals like adhesives, additives, catalysts constitute about 25.71 percent share and knowledge chemicals comprising agrochemicals, pharmaceuticals etc., have about 18 percent share of the industry. Since, India imports potash fertilisers, ethylene, propylene, polyethylene, polypropylene, vinyls and synthetic rubber, such joint ventures will be mutually profitable.

India's on-route location along major sea lanes and its emergence as a major refining hub can make it one of the strategic locations like Japan, South Korea for hiring of storage facilities and emergency stockpiling to manage the geopolitical risk in the Strait of Hormuz for Saudi Arabia as well as cater to India's concerns for energy security. India can develop new axis of energy cooperation with Saudi Arabia through swap trade with its oil and gas equity in East and South East Asia to serve the Saudi Arabia's customers in East Asia in exchange for equivalent exports from the Kingdom to India. The swap deal enables not only lower shipping costs for all parties but balances out regional differences in seasonal demand. It would also help the Saudi exporters to remain competitive in East Asia in the face of competing regional supplies from Russia.

Through technical agreements, India can benefit Saudi Arabia in many upstream operations. According to Platt Global E&P company list, Oil and Natural Gas Corporation (ONGC) ranked number two in the year 2012. It has successful drilling operations even in the most difficult terrain of Sakhalin in Russia and has set the world record on horizontal drilling. It has made advances in recent years in high technology drilling operations especially horizontal wells, multi lateral wells, acquired capability to drill through any geological formations and highly deviated oil wells. Its organic reserve replacement ratio is more impressive than most of its illustrious global counterparts. Along with Tata Energy Research Institute (TERI), it has developed microbes for microbial enhanced oil recovery technology, which can extract oil from less productive wells by injecting microbes that produce carbon dioxide and methane gases. Indian technology is superior to others as it developed microbes strong enough to survive in the extreme cold and heat of the desert as well as in salinity that is thrice that of sea water. It reduces the need for natural gas injection to maintain oil reservoir pressure in the maturing oil fields.

Indian companies have competence in manufacturing oil field and drilling equipments. Saudi Arabia's Al Qahtani Sons Group signed a joint venture with Indian firm Sledgehammer Oil Tools to build one of the largest manufacturing plants for oil field and drilling equipments in the Kingdom. Several other companies are keen to sign similar deals to expand their business in both the countries. As Saudi Arabia is also focusing on offshore oil exploration, there are possibilities of technical agreements with Indian companies, which have been providing offshore drilling support solutions. A biotechnology product 'Oilzapper', which is one of the most powerful bioremediation in the worldwide effort to tackle oil spill and oily sludge has been developed in India. In Kuwait, it has been successfully used.

India is setting new benchmarks in developing renewable and nuclear energy. It is the second biggest power producer from the renewable energy source with installation of over 13,200 mw capacity and constituting about 8 percent of its electricity supply. India has been ranked seventh worldwide for solar PV cell production and ninth rank in solar thermal power generation. It exports 75 percent of its production mainly to the European countries. Solar energy sector has received a tremendous boost under the Solar Mission Programme and is creating immense employment and business opportunities in India. There is ample scope for sharing of technology and best practices in the field of renewable energy.

Indian companies can promote energy efficiency operations and products in all its business and investment in Saudi Arabia especially in energy intensives industries like power, steel, aluminium, cement and water desalination. Today, India has some of the most energy efficient cement plants in the world. Countries like China, Germany, Turkey and Spain are importing power capacitors from India, which are being used to reduce the overall power factor of systems and are cheaper than other electrical equipments. Many Indian firms can provide fuel efficiency services, consultancy for energy audits, cogeneration, process optimisation, boiler efficiency and management of waste heat. Besides, India's green building movement, which started in early 2000s has created second largest space in the world under green building projects. There exist considerable opportunities for sharing of best practices in energy efficiency and conservation as well as in low carbon economy.

India-Saudi joint ventures in technology intensive manufacturing would further exploit their trade and investment complementarities. India is projected to export electrical and electronic goods worth up to $18 billion a year by 2015. Some Fortune 100 companies like Siemens source and manufacture electrical and electronic products in India for cost savings of 25 to 30 percent as compared to US and European levels. Joint ventures in Saudi Arabia and in India can build technical capabilities in the Kingdom as well as facilitate cheaper imports.

India has investment and business opportunities in many other sectors in Saudi Arabia. Indian construction companies with capabilities to build low cost housing projects and green buildings can create a niche for themselves in construction projects. In service sectors, IT, health care and tourism are beneficial for mutual business opportunities. Wipro Infotech has formed a joint venture with Dar Al Riyad Group called Wipro-Arabia Ltd to cater to Saudi IT market. Simultaneously, India provides a large number of tourists to Saudi Arabia annually. About 1.5 lakh pilgrims from India visit Saudi Arabia each year.

Vast opportunities in many sectors like pharmaceuticals, fertilizers, gems and jewelleries, vehicles etc remain unexploited. Besides, India can partner Saudi Arabia to cater to the growing export market of the WANA region for metallic products, machineries, electrical and electronic goods, automobiles and pharmaceuticals.

References

Al-Darwish, A, Alghaith, N and others, *Tackling Emerging Economic Challenges to Sustain Growth,* Washington DC, International Monetary Fund, 2015.

Almasoud, AH and Gandayh, Hatim M, 'Future of Solar Energy in Saudi Arabia', *Journal of King Saud University*, 2014, http://dx.doi.org/10.1016/j.jksues.2014.03.007.

Aljohani, Tawfiq M and Alzahrani, Abdullah M, 'The Operations of the GCCIA HVDC Project and Its Potential Impact on Electric Power Systems of the Region', *International Journal of Electronics and Electrical Engineering*, vol. 2, no. 3, September 2014, pp. 207-213.

Alshahrani, Saad and Alsadiq, Ali,' Economic Growth and Government Spending in Saudi Arabia: An Empirical Investigation', *IMF Working Paper,* WP/14/3, 2014, https://www.imf.org/external/pubs/ft/wp/2014/wp1403.pdf.

Aswathanarayana, U and Divi, Rao S, *Energy Portfolios,* Florida, CRC Press, 2009.

Chouhury, Nilima, 'ReneSola Enters Saudi Market with 15KW Contract', 14 January 2014, http://wwwtech.org/news/order_focus_renesola_enters_saudi_market_with_15kw_contract.

Cordemen Anthony H and Al Rodhan, Khalid R, *'The Changing Dynamics of Energy in the Middle East'*, Westport USA, Greenwood Publishing Group, 2006.

'Dubai Doubles Capacity of Mega Solar Park', *Gulf News*, 15 January 2015, http://gulfnews.com/news/gulf/uae/environment/dubai-doubles-capacity-of-mega-solar-park-1.1441860.

Fotuhi, Vahid, 'Concern over Saudi Arabia's Summer Diesel

Consumption Surge', *The National Business,* 5 July 2013, http://www.thenational.ae/business/industry-insights/energy/concern-over-saudi-arabias-summer-diesel-consumption-surge.

'GCC Energy Sector – Quarterly Review 2011', *Ventures Middle East,* 2011, http://www.pipelineme.com/media/797133/gcc-energy-december-2011.pdf.

'Greater Power Generation Key to Sustain Kingdom's Growth', *Arab News,* 15 December 2011, http://www.arabnews.com.

HOK, http://www.hok.com/about/news/2012/10/31/kapsarc-reaches-leed-for-homes-milestone.

Husain, Syed Rashid, 'KSA Shifting to Unconventional Gas Resources', Saudi Gazette, 3 August 2014, http://www.saudigazette.com.

KAUST, http://www.kaust.edu.sa/green-campus-sustainable-development.html.

International Trade Centre Database, http://www.intracen.org.

Mahdi, Wael 'Mecca Seeks to Lead Saudi Arabia's Solar Energy', *Bloomberg News,* 23 September 2012, http://www.bloomberg.com/news/2012-09-23/mecca-seeks-to-lead-saudi-arabia-s-solar-energy-expansion.html.

McCullough, DC, 'Saudi Arabia's Green Decree Brings Hopes of Sustainability', *The Guardian,* 12 May 2014, http://www.the.guardian.com.

O'Kane, Michael, *'Doing Business in Saudi Arabia'*, Tel Aviv, Al-Andalus Publishing, 2013.

'Refining Margins Under Pressure to 2015', *Hydrocarbon processing.com,* http://www.hydrocarbonprocessing.com/Article/2837639/Refining-margins-under-pressure-to-2015.html.

'Saudi Arabia Explores Potential $109 bn Solar Industry', *Al-Arabiya News,* 3 July 2013, httpwww.english.alarabia.net.

'Saudi Arabia Finds New Gas Fields in Red Sea', *Reuters,* 9 October 2012, http://www.reuters.com/article/2012/10/09/saudi-gas-discovery-idUSL6E8L9O3020121009.

'Saudi Arabia Powering Up', *Oxford Business Group,* 18 November 2014, http://www.oxfordbusinessgroup.com/news/saudi-arabia-powering.

'Saudi Arabia's ACWA Power Shifts toward Renewable Energy', *Emirates GBC Newsletter*, vol. IV, no. 11, 2014 http://emiratesgbc.org/newsletter/volume-iv-issue-11.

'KSA to Build 5 Solar Power Stations', *Saudi Gazette*, 22 September 2014, http://www.saudigazette.com.sa.

Shamseddine, Reem, 'Saudi Arabia, Kuwait Shared Zone Tensions underlie Oilfield Closure', *Reuters*, 21 October 2014, http://in.reuters.com/article/2014/10/21/saudi-kuwait-oil-disputes-idUSL6N0SF0BM20141021.

Shamseddine, Reem, 'Aramco Awards Midyan Gas Project to L&T', *Reuters*, 21 May 2013.

Shell Press Release, 2008, http://wwwshell.com/content/dam/shell/static/usa/downloads/press/2008-news.pdf.

'*The Report: Saudi Arabia 2013*', London, Oxford Business Group, 2013.

World Energy Resources 2013, 23rd edition, London, World Energy Council Publication, 2013, http://www.worldenergy.org.

Annexures

Table 1: Energy Products Exported by Saudi Arabia

Mineral fuels, oils, distillation products, etc — *Unit: US Dollar thousand*

Code	*Product label*	*Exported value in 2010*	*Exported value in 2011*	*Exported value in 2012*	*Exported value in 2013*
'2709	Crude petroleum oils	189433610	284976018	305237241	293994569
'2710	Petroleum oils, not crude	17955268	22972609	22731103	19060018
'2711	Petroleum gases	7050621	8176503	8155722	7848986
'2707	Oils & other products of the distillation of high temp coal tar etc	444838	784179	838358	733463
'2712	Petroleum jelly, mineral waxes & similar products	314510	644909	520037	291378
'2701	Coal, briquettes, ovoids & similar solid fuels manufactured from coal	0	400	323	409
'2704	Coke & semicoke of... coal, lignite, peat, retort carbon	0	213	172	133
'2703	Peat (incl peat litter), w/n agglomerated	0	0	0	23
'2708	Pitch & pitch coke, obtained from coal tar or from other mineral tars	0	0	0	0
'2702	Lignite w/n agglomerated, excl jet	0	0	207	0
'2713	Petroleum coke, petroleum bitumen & other residues of petroleum oils	49816	68852	829	0
'2714	Bitumen & asphalt, natural, shale & tar sands; asphaltites & asphaltic	0	0	0	0
	Total	215248663	317623683	337483992	321928979

Source: Calculated from International Trade Center (ITC) Datanase, Geneva.

Table 2: Energy Products Imported by Saudi Arabia

Mineral fuels, oils, distillation products, etc *Unit: US Dollar thousand*

Code	*Product label*	*Imported value in 2010*	*Imported value in 2011*	*Imported value in 2012*	*Imported value in 2013*
'2710	Petroleum oils, not crude	152598	244063	522094	1835598
'2713	Petroleum coke, petroleum bitumen & other residues of petroleum oils	14445	22791	49247	238102
'2701	Coal, briquettes, ovoids & similar solid fuels manu-factured from coal	26293	26615	33853	40398
'2707	Oils & other products of the distillation of high temp coal tar etc	16841	15557	11269	20207
'2704	Coke & semicoke of...coal, lignite, peat, retort carbon	15057	13077	18027	20020
'2708	Pitch & pitch coke, obtained from coal tar or from other mineral tars	0	0	3629	16454
'2712	Petroleum jelly, mineral waxes & similar products	11637	7221	8374	9397
'2703	Peat (incl peat litter), w/n agglomerated	4126	5154	8037	8923
'2714	Bitumen & asphalt, natural, shale & tar sands, asphaltites & asphaltic	0	0	13603	2951
'2702	Lignite w/n agglomerated, excl jet	1047	0	329	2314
'2706	Tar distilled from coal, lignite or peat & other mineral tars etc	541	979	1506	1288
'2711	Petroleum gases	663	0	491	807
'2715	Bituminous mixtures from... natural asphalt, natural & petroleum bitumen	561	771	1004	220
	Total	243809	336228	671463	2196679

Source: Calculated from ITC

Table 3: Supplying Markets for Energy Products Imported by Saudi Arabia

Mineral fuels, oils, distillation products, etc *Unit: US Dollar thousand*

Exporters	*Imported value in 2010*	*% share 2010*	*Imported value in 2013*	*% share in 2013*
Total	1863384		10907248	
India	670013	36.0	6877519	63.1
Italy	125600	6.7	1104781	10.1
Oman	25045	1.3	540957	5.0
Singapore	199267	10.7	390972	3.6
Greece	6011	0.3	389896	3.6
Taipei, Chinese	127480	6.8	289597	2.7
Belgium	29521	1.6	272007	2.5
Netherlands	163666	8.8	219964	2.0
Korea, Republic of	9483	0.5	130370	1.2
United States of America	31843	1.7	113260	1.0
Russian Federation	56	0.0	77628	0.7
France	26197	1.4	75523	0.7
Malaysia	2372	0.1	65207	0.6
Qatar	206000	11.1	56769	0.5

Source: Calculated from ITC.

Table 4: Importing Markets for Energy Products Exported by Saudi Arabia

Mineral fuels, oils, distillation products, etc			*Unit: US Dollar thousand*	
Importers	*Exported value in 2010*	*% share 2010*	*Exported value in 2013*	*% share in 2013*
Total	203785462		312018173	
United States of America	31674468	15.5	51883151	16.6
Japan	35449822	17.4	49012861	15.7
China	25868002	12.7	43307121	13.9
Korea, Republic of	25968698	12.7	36127246	11.6
India	17948861	8.8	32933978	10.6
Taipei, Chinese	10651540	5.2	13606355	4.4
Singapore	8864742	4.4	9540462	3.1
France	3265583	1.6	7725616	2.5
South Africa	2756304	1.4	7553671	2.4
Thailand	4844926	2.4	7331488	2.3
Spain	4247409	2.1	7101464	2.3
Italy	3384493	1.7	6225473	2.0
Indonesia	3624641	1.8	5557473	1.8
Netherlands	2564972	1.3	4474992	1.4
Brazil	1974542	1.0	3009327	1.0
Pakistan	2953342	1.4	2916855	0.9
Philippines	2403985	1.2	2802363	0.9
Jordan	2020652	1.0	2769350	0.9
Canada	1908332	0.9	2610036	0.8
United Kingdom	292226	0.1	2388958	0.8
Morocco	1646524	0.8	2173999	0.7
Germany	404871	0.2	1728163	0.6
Malaysia	1742433	0.9	1569030	0.5
Egypt	1092584	0.5	1459979	0.5
Greece	1386811	0.7	1361059	0.4
Oman	102592	0.1	1167612	0.4

Source: Calculated from ITC.

Table 5: Products Exported by Saudi Arabia
Unit: US Dollar thousand

Code	*Product label*	*Exported value in 2010*	*% share in 2010*	*Exported value in 2013*	*% share 2013*
Total	All products	251143033		375396586	
'27	Mineral fuels, oils, distillation products, etc	215248664	85.71	321928979	85.8
'39	Plastics and articles thereof	11339317	4.52	17029840	4.5
'29	Organic chemicals	7440552	2.96	13210626	3.5
'89	Ships, boats and other floating structures	631623	0.25	2239937	0.6
'28	Inorganic chemicals, precious metal compound, isotopes	310337	0.12	1711297	0.5
'85	Electrical, electronic equipment	1058756	0.42	1560284	0.4
'84	Machinery, nuclear reactors, boilers, etc	1507780	0.60	1475217	0.4
'87	Vehicles other than railway, tramway	1218165	0.49	1277500	0.3
'04	Dairy products, eggs, honey, edible animal product nes	918577	0.37	1138708	0.3
'76	Aluminium and articles thereof	517502	0.21	1038960	0.3
'31	Fertilizers	1250862	0.50	1037929	0.3

Source: Calculated from ITC.

Table 6: Importing Markets for Products Exported by Saudi Arabia Unit: US Dollar thousand

S.No.	*Importers*	*Exported value in 2010*	*% share in 2010*	*Exported value in 2013*	*% share 2013*
	Total	240786089		357680288	
1	China	32829048	13.6	53450711	14.9
2	United States of America	32650735	13.6	53098032	14.8
3	Japan	35972010	14.9	49856199	13.9
4	Korea, Republic of	26820002	11.1	37665214	10.5
5	India	20374084	8.5	36596585	10.2
6	Taipei, Chinese	11880553	4.9	15569178	4.4
7	Singapore	11233332	4.7	12862429	3.6
8	Thailand	5646047	2.3	8405097	2.3
9	France	3531691	1.5	8065847	2.3
10	South Africa	3239641	1.3	8026551	2.2
11	Spain	4691313	1.9	7762513	2.2
12	Italy	4287871	1.8	7305350	2.0
13	Indonesia	4360840	1.8	6526424	1.8
14	Netherlands	3150532	1.3	5033211	1.4
15	Jordan	3024141	1.3	4019283	1.1
16	Pakistan	3837918	1.6	3847222	1.1
17	Brazil	2059255	0.9	3194222	0.9
18	Egypt	2120138	0.9	3042520	0.9
19	United Kingdom	771417	0.3	3027609	0.8
20	Philippines	2452187	1.0	2866457	0.8
21	Morocco	2107916	0.9	2812808	0.8
22	Canada	1964820	0.8	2631715	0.7
23	Germany	845493	0.4	2254661	0.6
24	Oman	626190	0.3	2023711	0.6

Source: Calculated from ITC

Table 7: Products Imported by Saudi Arabia
Unit: US Dollar thousand

Code	*Product label*	*Imported value in 2009*	*% share in 2009*	*Imported value in 2013*	*% share 2013*
Total	All products	95552181		163712750	
'84	Machinery, nuclear reactors, boilers, etc	6011368	6.3	26092366	15.9
'87	Vehicles other than railway, tramway	10594219	11.1	23449859	14.3
'85	Electrical, electronic equipment	4479798	4.7	17724813	10.8
'73	Articles of iron or steel	1819310	1.9	7591877	4.6
'10	Cereals	3382928	3.5	6049621	3.7
'72	Iron and steel	1111176	1.2	5998907	3.7
'30	Pharmaceutical products	2380722	2.5	5122546	3.1
'71	Pearls, precious stones, metals, coins, etc	680039	0.7	5068070	3.1
'90	Optical, photo, technical, medical, etc apparatus	62497	0.1	3702245	2.3
'39	Plastics and articles thereof	310246	0.3	3387376	2.1
'74	Copper and articles thereof	1022711	1.1	3271166	2.0
'02	Meat and edible meat offal	1476262	1.5	2780296	1.7
'94	Furniture, lighting, signs, prefabricated buildings	156545	0.2	2384391	1.5
'76	Aluminium and articles thereof	706426	0.7	2359231	1.4
'40	Rubber and articles thereof	816819	0.9	2325667	1.4
'62	Articles of apparel, accessories, not knit or crochet	529006	0.6	2215129	1.4
'27	Mineral fuels, oils, distillation products, etc	8740	0.0	2196679	1.3
'29	Organic chemicals	432919	0.5	2186357	1.3
'38	Miscellaneous chemical products	405427	0.4	2046166	1.2
'04	Dairy products, eggs, honey, edible animal product nes	909220	1.0	1967560	1.2

Source: Calculated from ITC.

Table 8: Supplying Markets for Products Imported by Saudi Arabia Unit: US Dollar thousand

Exporters	*Imported value in 2010*	*% share in 2010*	*Imported value in 2013*	*% share 2013*
Total	94237535		143616980	
United States of America	11590302	12.3	18988191	13.2
China	10366445	11.0	18739814	13.0
Germany	7645909	8.1	12364342	8.6
India	4483704	4.8	12357201	8.6
Korea, Republic of	4556673	4.8	8827722	6.1
Japan	6486304	6.9	6847345	4.8
United Kingdom	4757624	5.0	6600495	4.6
Italy	3531983	3.7	5902880	4.1
France	5190531	5.5	4536391	3.2
Turkey	2219407	2.4	3191538	2.2
Spain	1386212	1.5	3154683	2.2
Thailand	2118026	2.2	2980553	2.1
Netherlands	2215884	2.4	2953835	2.1
Brazil	3097368	3.3	2838775	2.0
Belgium	1358714	1.4	2452847	1.7
Oman	690535	0.7	2363384	1.6
Switzerland	1568789	1.7	2317603	1.6
Egypt	1548992	1.6	1975234	1.4

Source: Calculated from ITC.

Table 9: Saudi Arabia's Exports to West Asia (WA) Unit: US Dollar thousand

Product code	Product lable	Saudi Arabia's Exports to WANA		WA Imports from world			
		Value in 2013	% share in 2013	Value in 2011	% share 2011	Value in 2013	% share 2013
TOTAL	All products	19504601		962196095		1031678632	
'39	Plastics and articles thereof	4375469	22.4	32356029	3.4	35122050	3.4
'89	Ships, boats and other floating structures	2105448	10.8	5636030	0.6	9122336	0.9
'85	Electrical, electronic equipment	1227765	6.3	82334729	8.6	88611935	8.6
'04	Dairy products, eggs, honey, edible animal product nes	1068581	5.5	7130480	0.7	8100033	0.8
'29	Organic chemicals	895334	4.6	15502686	1.6	16023636	1.6
'87	Vehicles other than railway, tramway	885412	4.5	76987363	8.0	93363291	9.0
'84	Machinery, nuclear reactors, boilers, etc	825639	4.2	117630146	12.2	121584858	11.8
'73	Articles of iron or steel	733579	3.8	25457520	2.6	29302190	2.8
'48	Paper and paperboard, articles of pulp, paper and board	639313	3.3	11720039	1.2	11587053	1.1
'72	Iron and steel	516682	2.6	51651034	5.4	43142584	4.2
'34	Soaps, lubricants, waxes, candles, modelling pastes	480149	2.5	3283719	0.3	4115591	0.4
'19	Cereal, flour, starch, milk preparations and products	464719	2.4	3555161	0.4	4411007	0.4
'71	Pearls, precious stones, metals, coins, etc	431089	2.2	60699651	6.3	80104423	7.8

'76	Aluminium and articles thereof	430938	2.2	9598787	1.0	10546643	1.0
'20	Vegetable, fruit, nut, etc food preparations	376684	1.9	2699197	0.3	3078857	0.3
'33	Essential oils, perfumes, cosmetics, toileteries	315755	1.6	6740259	0.7	7837874	0.8
'30	Pharmaceutical products	299855	1.5	18592088	1.9	21427581	2.1
'96	Miscellaneous manufactured articles	257498	1.3	1741627	0.2	3116716	0.3
'15	Animal,vegetable fats and oils, cleavage products, etc	244717	1.3	10088349	1.0	9552887	0.9
'32	Tanning, dyeing extracts, tannins, derivs, pigments etc	227318	1.2	5044340	0.5	5305946	0.5
'38	Miscellaneous chemical products	216020	1.1	8987118	0.9	9029331	0.9
'17	Sugars and sugar confectionery	194180	1.0	6716528	0.7	5461412	0.5
'22	Beverages, spirits and vinegar	181933	0.9	2620942	0.3	3079266	0.3
'28	Inorganic chemicals, precious metal compound, isotopes	172260	0.9	5656693	0.6	5705477	0.6
'68	Stone, plaster, cement, asbestos, mica, etc articles	161053	0.8	3080809	0.3	3957416	0.4
'08	Edible fruit, nuts, peel of citrus fruit, melons	144661	0.7	5828591	0.6	5558059	0.5
'70	Glass and glassware	139090	0.7	3738568	0.4	4008089	0.4
'94	Furniture, lighting, signs, prefabricated buildings	80864	0.4	8977180	0.9	12594022	1.2
'02	Meat and edible meat offal	79653	0.4	9366501	1.0	9628645	0.9
'90	Optical, photo, technical, medical, etc						

	apparatus	68860	0.4	16206184	1.7	18836527	1.8
'07	Edible vegetables and certain roots and tubers	66164	0.3	3915962	0.4	3730194	0.4
'69	Ceramic products	61534	0.3	4212411	0.4	4946924	0.5
'21	Miscellaneous edible preparations	48573	0.2	4049074	0.4	4464950	0.4
'40	Rubber and articles thereof	43728	0.2	11954468	1.2	11528756	1.1
'62	Articles of apparel, accessories, not knit or crochet	40701	0.2	8811479	0.9	10514930	1.0
'27	Mineral fuels, oils, distillation products, etc	39491	0.2	133214610	13.8	124782797	12.1
'31	Fertilizers	36751	0.2	2321801	0.2	2397665	0.2

Source: Calculated from ITC.

Table 10: Importing Markets from West Asia for Products Exported by Saudi Arabia Unit: US Dollar thousand

Importers	*Exported value in 2010*	*% share 2010*	*Exported value in 2013*	*% share 2013*
Total	240786089		357680288	
Middle East Aggregation	11901858	4.9	13647824	3.8
Jordan	3024141	1.3	4019283	1.1
Egypt	2120138	0.9	3042520	0.9
Oman	626190	0.3	2023711	0.6
Turkey	2437156	1.0	2014870	0.6
Qatar	1222413	0.5	1218806	0.3
Yemen	567304	0.2	843613	0.2
Lebanon	406764	0.2	440218	0.1
Palestine, State of	11117	0.0	43997	0.0
Israel	560	0.0	806	0.0

Source: Calculated From ITC.

Table 11: Saudi Arabia's Imports from West Asia (WA) Unit: US Dollar thousand

Product code	*Product lable*	*Saudi Arabia's Imports from WA*				*WA Exports to world*			
		Value in 2011	*% share in 2011*	*Value in 2013*	*% share 2013*	*Value in 2011*	*% share 2011*	*Value in 2013*	*% share 2013*
Total	All products	14468198		19910756		1335396568		1329065245	
'72	Iron and steel	2358496	16.3	2623437	13.2	22404918	1.7	17241263	1.3
'74	Copper and articles thereof	669009	4.6	1396130	7.0	5236672	0.4	6105495	0.5
'76	Aluminium and articles thereof	895315	6.2	1286305	6.5	13827163	1.0	15724417	1.2
'71	Pearls, precious stones, metals, coins, etc	597974	4.1	1266759	6.4	60519396	4.5	59509492	4.5
'73	Articles of iron or steel	617240	4.3	1160296	5.8	11494670	0.9	11170944	0.8
'85	Electrical, electronic equipment	676839	4.7	1019407	5.1	26269399	2.0	25178998	1.9
'84	Machinery, nuclear reactors, boilers, etc	492114	3.4	870351	4.4	27850464	2.1	23857763	1.8
'39	Plastics and articles thereof	617395	4.3	862660	4.3	36018590	2.7	41934916	3.2
'26	Ores, slag and ash	267572	1.8	614495	3.1	5355761	0.4	6483257	0.5
'04	Dairy products, eggs, honey, edible animal product nes	512938	3.5	587546	3.0	3617631	0.3	3435278	0.3
'30	Pharmaceutical products	387239	2.7	468913	2.4	9522351	0.7	8993710	0.7
'94	Furniture, lighting, signs, prefabricated buildings	217280	1.5	368753	1.9	3675940	0.3	4469555	0.3
'48	Paper and paperboard, articles of pulp, paper and board	288974	2.0	343529	1.7	4660738	0.3	3232126	0.2

'27	Mineral fuels, oils, distillation products, etc	96248	0.7	339247	1.7	905931574	67.8	899408488	67.7
'08	Edible fruit, nuts, peel of citrus fruit, melons	321441	2.2	315681	1.6	8381722	0.6	7395354	0.6
'25	Salt, sulphur, earth, stone, plaster, lime and cement	90872	0.6	297040	1.5	7549247	0.6	6974396	0.5
'69	Ceramic products	225500	1.6	277709	1.4	2198763	0.2	2287528	0.2
'18	Cocoa and cocoa preparations	214114	1.5	276374	1.4	997890	0.1	1149316	0.1
'07	Edible vegetables and certain roots and tubers	274313	1.9	268098	1.3	4332767	0.3	3725726	0.3
'15	Animal, vegetable fats and oils, cleavage products, etc	409529	2.8	267521	1.3	3754119	0.3	2870295	0.2
'70	Glass and glassware	203253	1.4	252059	1.3	2647994	0.2	2352021	0.2
'17	Sugars and sugar confectionery	207248	1.4	248412	1.2	2502572	0.2	1970305	0.1
'57	Carpets and other textile floor coverings	143056	1.0	240677	1.2	3254233	0.2	3082173	0.2
'38	Miscellaneous chemical products	193342	1.3	228819	1.1	6949953	0.5	7616237	0.6
'33	Essential oils, perfumes, cosmetics, toileteries	178524	1.2	226788	1.1	2016701	0.2	2679197	0.2
'19	Cereal, flour, starch, milk preparations and products	190757	1.3	222015	1.1	2445053	0.2	2916188	0.2
'29	Organic chemicals	145512	1.0	163305	0.8	25729860	1.9	27444102	2.1
'89	Ships, boats and other floating structures	383271	2.6	158382	0.8	3408519	0.3	5527703	0.4
'87	Vehicles other than railway, tramway	183714	1.3	150959	0.8	24124014	1.8	24986439	1.9

Source: Calculated from ITC.

Table 12: Supplying Countries from West Asia for Products Imported by Saudi Arabia Unit: US Dollar thousand

Importers	*Imported value in 2010*	*% share 2010*	*Imported value in 2013*	*% share 2013*
Total	94237535		143616980	
West Asian Aggregation	8474850	9.0	10204552	7.1
Turkey	2219407	2.4	3191538	2.2
Oman	690535	0.7	2363384	1.6
Egypt	1548992	1.6	1975234	1.4
Qatar	1065449	1.1	1136045	0.8
Jordan	661698	0.7	963295	0.7
Lebanon	246013	0.3	346950	0.2
Yemen	205379	0.2	219565	0.2
Palestine, State of	5653	0.0	8428	0.0
Israel	227	0.0	113	0.0
Bahrain	1159643	1.2		
Iran (Islamic Republic of)	129250	0.1		

Source: Calculated from ITC.

Table 13: India's Imports from Saudi Arabia Unit: US Dollor thousand

Product code	Product lable	India's imports from Saudi Arabia				Saudi Arabia's exports to world				India's imports from world			
		Value in 2011	% share in 2011	Value in 2013	% share 2013	Value in 2011	% share 2011	Value in 2013	% share 2013	Value in 2011	% share 2011	Value in 2013	% share 2013
TOTAL	All products	28423659		36596585		364697697		375396586		462402791		466045567	
'27	Mineral fuels, oils, distillation products, etc	25524571	89.8	32933978	90.0	317623681	87.1	321928979	85.8	157356407	34.0	184194009	39.5
'29	Organic chemicals	1145402	4.0	1176784	3.2	12135180	3.3	13210626	3.5	14028692	3.0	16960213	3.6
'39	Plastics and articles thereof	484236	1.7	800490	2.2	14505129	4.0	17029840	4.5	7999615	1.7	9984763	2.1
'31	Fertilizers	176123	0.6	403615	1.1	1615783	0.4	1037929	0.3	8711778	1.9	5958024	1.3
'28	Inorganic chemicals, precious metal compound, isotopes	342914	1.2	336673	0.9	633903	0.2	1711297	0.5	5357327	1.2	5100315	1.1
'76	Aluminium and articles thereof	158240	0.6	188512	0.5	517140	0.1	1038960	0.3	2834980	0.6	3177639	0.7
'74	Copper and articles thereof	76326	0.3	151412	0.4	78204	0.0	471264	0.1	2602773	0.6	2817308	0.6
'38	Miscellaneous chemical products	43772	0.2	106144	0.3	522210	0.1	805743	0.2	3640605	0.8	3843405	0.8
'71	Pearls, precious stones, metals, coins, etc	13645	0.0	93450	0.3	1032831	0.3	802807	0.2	93596866	20.2	67499912	14.5
'72	Iron and steel	157290	0.6	87682	0.2	824166	0.2	739987	0.2	12945475	2.8	10118914	2.2
'25	Salt, sulphur, earth, stone, plaster, lime and cement	22797	0.1	53575	0.1	256233	0.1	129397	0.0	2841937	0.6	2379016	0.5
'32	Tanning, dyeing extracts, tannins, derivs, pigments etc	22385	0.1	38085	0.1	443030	0.1	402893	0.1	1412667	0.3	1517464	0.3
'84	Machinery, nuclear reactors, boilers, etc	22782	0.1	8434	0.0	1644603	0.5	1475217	0.4	35489437	7.7	31945783	6.9

'73	Articles of iron or steel	7798	0.0	3285	0.0	1037069	0.3	860260	0.2	4458639	1.0	3752243	0.8
'89	Ships, boats and other floating structures	0	0.0	1351	0.0	1200485	0.3	2239937	0.6	3352906	0.7	7004947	1.5
'48	Paper and paperboard, articles of pulp, paper and board	6203	0.0	865	0.0	1109604	0.3	768025	0.2	2454712	0.5	2376762	0.5
'85	Electrical, electronic equipment	7046	0.0	830	0.0	1187122	0.3	1560284	0.4	32261003	7.0	29790256	6.4

Source: Calculated from ITC.

Table 14: Saudi Arabia's Imports From India Unit: US Dollar thousand

Product code	Product lable	*Saudi Arabia's imports from India* Value in 2011	% share in 2011	Value in 2013	% share 2013	*India's exports to world* Value in 2011	% share 2011	Value in 2013	% share 2013	*Saudi Arabia's imports from world* Value in 2011	% share 2011	Value in 2013	% share 2013
TOTAL	All products	4231442		5771803		301483250		336611389		131586578		163712750	
'10	Cereals	787754	18.6	1040232	18.0	5371013	1.8	11592455	3.4	4362664	3.3	6049621	3.7
'85	Electrical, electronic equipment	447290	10.6	604849	10.5	11744262	3.9	11275864	3.3	14669940	11.1	17724813	10.8
'84	Machinery, nuclear reactors, boilers, etc	321522	7.6	530769	9.2	10752338	3.6	13126148	3.9	20518959	15.6	26092366	15.9
'72	Iron and steel	230266	5.4	344095	6.0	7925589	2.6	10206482	3.0	6122000	4.7	5998907	3.7
'29	Organic chemicals	211927	5.0	306854	5.3	11145939	3.7	13340364	4.0	2104987	1.6	2186357	1.3
'62	Articles of apparel, accessories, not knit or crochet	205289	4.9	302612	5.2	7937483	2.6	8743400	2.6	1838667	1.4	2215129	1.4
'02	Meat and edible meat offal	238492	5.6	282835	4.9	2686670	0.9	4770622	1.4	2532838	1.9	2780296	1.7
'73	Articles of iron or steel	183275	4.3	280734	4.9	6501245	2.2	7347626	2.2	5363948	4.1	7591877	4.6
'87	Vehicles other than railway, tramway	58506	1.4	192589	3.3	10280635	3.4	13800069	4.1	16664532	12.7	23449859	14.3
'33	Essential oils, perfumes, cosmetics, toileteries	123512	2.9	122486	2.1	1234867	0.4	1619624	0.5	1321457	1.0	1570298	1.0
'27	Mineral fuels, oils, distillation products,	31186	0.7	116407	2.0	56556789	18.8	69571281	20.7	336229	0.3	2196679	1.3
'25	Salt, sulphur, earth, stone, plaster, lime and cement	47313	1.1	103542	1.8	1599461	0.5	2037435	0.6	272541	0.2	571011	0.3
'39	Plastics and articles thereof	92804	2.2	92074	1.6	5465281	1.8	6222703	1.8	2891124	2.2	3387376	2.1
'09	Coffee, tea, mate and spices	97891	2.3	90737	1.6	2972220	1.0	2885200	0.9	745574	0.6	709953	0.4

'08	Edible fruit, nuts, peel of citrus fruit,	62070	1.5	89136	1.5	1448995	0.5	1676457	0.5	1031898	0.8	1190190	0.7
'61	Articles of apparel, accessories, knit	103780	2.5	85802	1.5	5807252	1.9	6959257	2.1	890849	0.7	811720	0.5
'17	Sugars and sugar confectionery	53064	1.3	77814	1.3	2075113	0.7	1179991	0.4	999623	0.8	1050849	0.6
'38	Miscellaneous chemical products	58101	1.4	73337	1.3	2521021	0.8	3398007	1.0	1901023	1.4	2046166	1.2
'40	Rubber and articles thereof	60641	1.4	66411	1.2	2583697	0.9	2974672	0.9	2067765	1.6	2325667	1.4
'20	Vegetable, fruit, nut, etc food preparations	67534	1.6	59387	1.0	355672	0.1	461858	0.1	792608	0.6	947777	0.6
'04	Dairy products, eggs, honey, edible animal product nes	7650	0.2	51039	0.9	222502	0.1	737603	0.2	1875258	1.4	1967560	1.2
'24	Tobacco and manufactured tobacco substitutes	25663	0.6	46710	0.8	797927	0.3	1084694	0.3	800563	0.6	1011750	0.6
'69	Ceramic products	18024	0.4	46080	0.8	363804	0.1	559327	0.2	797734	0.6	1040694	0.6
'64	Footwear, gaiters and the llike, parts thereof	23765	0.6	36588	0.6	2090537	0.7	2609804	0.8	517342	0.4	684218	0.4
'28	Inorganic chemicals, precious metal compound, isotopes	32690	0.8	34834	0.6	1409322	0.5	1466232	0.4	730472	0.6	936679	0.6
'74	Copper and articles thereof	94520	2.2	31682	0.5	2959274	1.0	3066552	0.9	2995037	2.3	3271166	2.0
'48	Paper and paperboard, articles of pulp, paper and board	27697	0.7	30479	0.5	906989	0.3	1141261	0.3	1740614	1.3	1783466	1.1
'71	Pearls, precious stones, metals, coins, etc	38595	0.9	30168	0.5	50015590	16.6	44157662	13.1	2460122	1.9	5068070	3.1
'68	Stone, plaster, cement, asbestos, mica, etc articles	11703	0.3	28475	0.5	1017412	0.3	1390707	0.4	475033	0.4	591979	0.4
'32	Tanning, dyeing extracts,												

	tannins, derivs,pigments etc	30544	0.7	27870	0.5	1918192	0.6	2616524	0.8	620447	0.5	647609	0.4
'90	Optical, photo, technical, medical, etc apparatus	19380	0.5	27821	0.5	1794909	0.6	2288877	0.7	2579616	2.0	3702245	2.3
'26	Ores, slag and ash	13235	0.3	21065	0.4	4918406	1.6	2388949	0.7	1848049	1.4	1380347	0.8
'94	Furniture, lighting, signs, prefabricated buildings	12692	0.3	20844	0.4	901083	0.3	1193881	0.4	1664261	1.3	2384391	1.5
'12	Oil seed, oleagic fruits, grain, seed, fruit, etc, nes	10161	0.2	17960	0.3	1853859	0.6	1880345	0.6	625947	0.5	747520	0.5
'76	Aluminium and articles thereof	19280	0.5	16737	0.3	1423415	0.5	2078003	0.6	1887947	1.4	2359231	1.4
'44	Wood and articles of wood, wood charcoal	6453	0.2	10084	0.2	220652	0.1	351497	0.1	1331244	1.0	1496778	0.9
'19	Cereal, flour, starch, milk preparations and products	5679	0.1	9785	0.2	368419	0.1	491187	0.1	956523	0.7	1142319	0.7
'30	Pharmaceutical products	2971	0.1	5398	0.1	8259853	2.7	11731941	3.5	3753668	2.9	5122546	3.1
'15	Animal,vegetable fats and oils, cleavage products, etc	3999	0.1	4652	0.1	1048593	0.3	984201	0.3	1123045	0.9	952301	0.6
'01	Live animals	0	0.0	625	0.0	13153	0.0	12504	0.0	655644	0.5	968379	0.6
'89	Ships, boats and other floating structures	161	0.0	157	0.0	7048272	2.3	3597492	1.1	856496	0.7	1946264	1.2
'88	Aircraft, spacecraft, and parts thereof	0	0.0	0	0.0	2302532	0.8	4151795	1.2	1790092	1.4	1661046	1.0

Source: Calculated from ITC.

Table 15: India's Energy Imports from Saudi Arabia Unit: US Dollar thousand

Product code	Product label	*India's Imports from Saudi Arabia*		*Saudi Arabia's Exports to world*		*India's Imports from world*	
		Value in 2011	*Value in 2013*	*Value in 2011*	*Value in 2013*	*Value in 2011*	*Value in 2013*
'2709	Crude petroleum oils	23513374	31202907	284976018	293994569	122125544	148046659
'2711	Petroleum gases	1775678	1660999	8176503	7848986	11023750	14272701
'2710	Petroleum oils, not crude	229495	69901	22972609	19060018	7353268	4419444
'2712	Petroleum jelly, mineral waxes & similar products	2946	0	644909	291378	120347	156305
'2713	Petroleum coke, petroleum bitumen & other residues of petroleum oils	67	0	68852	0	883574	1281330
'2701	Coal; briquettes, ovoids & similar solid fuels manufactured from coal	2686	0	400	409	14623238	14931194
'2704	Coke & semicoke of...coal, lignite, peat, retort carbon	0	0	213	133	983391	846980
'2707	Oils & other products of the distillation of high temp coal tar etc	1		784179	733463	201772	184490

Source: ITC

Table 16: India's Energy Exports to Saudi Arabia Unit: US Dollar thousand

Product code	*Product label*	*India's Exports to Saudi Arabia*		*Saudi Arabia's Imports from world*		*India's Exports to world*	
		Value in 2011	*Value in 2013*	*Value in 2011*	*Value in 2013*	*Value in 2011*	*Value in 2013*
'2710	Petroleum oils, not crude	1209240	6818371	244063	1835598	54611076	67075186
'2713	Petroleum coke, petroleum bitumen & other residues of petroleum oils	14428	32749	22791	238102	211993	283395
'2707	Oils & other products of the distillation of high temp coal tar etc	13726	23857	15557	20207	831759	1599240
'2712	Petroleum jelly; mineral waxes & similar products	1212	2086	7221	9397	84505	76329
'2704	Coke & semicoke of..coal, lignite, peat; retort carbon	89	456	13077	20020	276929	29203
'2706	Tar distilled from coal, lignite or peat & other mineral tars etc	221	0	979	1288	1004	880
'2701	Coal; briquettes, ovoids & similar solid fuels manufactured from coal	152	0	26615	40398	297726	154673
'2702	Lignite w/n agglomerated, excl jet	588	0	0	2314	1069	2725
'2703	Peat (incl peat litter), w/n agglomerated	0	0	5154	8923	84	10671
'2708	Pitch & pitch coke, obtained from coal tar or from other mineral tars	15	0	0	16454	27030	15702
'2711	Petroleum gases	0	0	0	807	193959	317519
'2714	Bitumen & asphalt, natural; shale & tar sands; asphaltites & asphaltic	0	0	0	2951	2915	4178
'2715	Bituminous mixtures from..natural asphalt, natural & petroleum bitumen	2	0	771	220	1237	1561
	Total	1239673	6877519	336228	2196679	56541286	69571262

Source: Calculated from ITC.

Table 17: Outward Investment of Saudi Arabia in Developing Countries (values in US$ million)

Industry	*No. of parent Company*	*No. of Affi-liates*	*Sales*	*Leading Parent Company*	*Leading Host Country*
Total (merchandise and services)	83	165	193,403	SABIC	UAE
Wholesale and retail trade	33	48	71,366	SABIC	UAE
Business activities	18	28	1,053	SABIC	Turkey
Finance	9	10	10,881	The National Commercial Bank	Bahrain
Electrical and electronic equipment	9	14	5,084	Saudi Cables Company	Turkey
Chemicals and chemical products	9	21	10,197	SABIC	Brazil
Transport, storage and communications	8	16	104,975	Saudi Oger Company Ltd	Turkey
Motor vehicles and other transport equipment	7	9	4,687	SABIC	Turkey
Other manufacturing	6	6	1,166	Al Muhaideb for Trading and Contracting Company	Turkey
Other services	6	6	17,297	Saudi Cables Company	Turkey
Textiles, clothing and leather	5	7	2,454	SABIC	Turkey
Construction	4	5	5,193	Zamil Industrial Investment Company	UAE
Wood and wood products	3	3	179	SABIC	Turkey
Machinery and equipment	3	3	1,072.00	Arabian Thermal Aire Industries Limited	Turkey

Non-metallic mineral products	2	2		Al Muhaideb for Trading and Contracting Company	India
Community, social and personal service activities	2	3	60	Ara Group International Holding Ltd	UAE
Precision instruments	1	1		Triad Condas International	Lebanon
Agriculture and hunting	1	1	43.5	Arabian Farms Development Company Ltd	UAE
Forestry and Fishing	1	1		Al Amin for Medical & Scientific Equipment	UAE
Education	1	1		Khalifa A Algosaibi Holding Co.	Bahrain

Source: ITC Database.